YOUR WORD
In
My Heart

Developing Deeper Intimacy with God

DEBRA-KAY WILLIAMS

YOUR WORD IN MY HEART. Copyright © 2021. Debra-Kay Williams. All Rights Reserved.

Printed in the United States of America.

No portion of this book may be reproduced, stored in a retrieval system, or transmitted in any form or by any means, except for brief quotations in printed reviews, without the prior written permission of DayeLight Publishers or Debra-Kay Williams.

Published by

ISBN: 978-1-953759-33-7 (paperback)

Scripture quotations marked "KJV" are taken from the Holy Bible, King James Version (Public Domain).

Scripture quotations marked "NKJV" are taken from the New King James Version. Copyright © 1982 by Thomas Nelson, Inc. Used by permission. All rights reserved. Bible text from the New King James Version® is not to be reproduced in copies or otherwise by any means except as permitted in writing by Thomas Nelson, Inc., Attn: Bible Rights and Permissions, P.O. Box 141000, Nashville, TN 37214-1000.

Dedication

To the living Word, Jesus Christ, my Savior and King, the true Author who inspired me to write this book.

To every young woman who wants to develop a deep relationship with God.

To every growing believer who wants to develop a deep relationship with God.

Acknowledgments

To my God, Father, and King, thank You for making the provision through Jesus Christ for my sins so I could enter a relationship with You. I thank You for endowing me with Your Holy Spirit, propelling me into purpose and the fulfillment of Your desires in my life. I thank You for being my constant Defender and Friend Who has blocked every weapon that the enemy has formed against my life. Thank You for allowing me to be born in this time and season where I can witness the manifestation of Your glory in the earth. Thank You, the true Author Who gave me the inspiration, wisdom, words, strength, and provision that I needed to complete this book. May Your glory live on eternally through the scriptures that are quoted in this book.

To my family, thank you for constantly supporting all my endeavours. Thank you for encouraging me and covering me in prayer. I thank The Lord for placing me in this family to fulfill His purpose.

To my friends, thank you for being faithful and being a great support system. Thank you for praying for me and being there when I need help.

To my ministry family and partners, thank you for pouring into my life so I could pour into others. Thank you for being a great counsel to me and for the warm fellowship and lasting friendships.

To Crystal Daye and the DayeLight Publisher's team, thank you for being a big help in making this book come to life; thank you for your guidance and all your great work.

Table of Contents

Dedication……………………………………iii
Acknowledgements ……………………… v
Introduction……………………………… 1
Preface ……………………………………… 3

HAVE A RELATIONSHIP WITH GOD

Chapter One
First Thing: Seek And Find …………… 9

Chapter Two
To Pray Or Not To Pray …………… 15

Chapter Three
Obedience, God's Love Language ……. 31

Chapter Four
True Intimacy ………………………… 39

Going Deeper

Chapter Five
How Much Do You Know The Word?.. 59

Chapter Six
Fasting, Is This Necessary?................. 67

Chapter Seven
Loving God 75

Chapter Eight
Do You Fear God?................................ 81

Daily Steps

Chapter Nine
Make Time To Meet With God............ 89

Chapter Ten
Give Yourself To Him 99

Appendix.. 107
References 109
About the Author................................111

Introduction

Hiding God's Word in our hearts is key to living in His will and desire for us. He is the Living Word, and if we want to get to know Him and have a relationship with Him, we must begin there. All scripture is God-breathed and is critical in teaching us about Him and what He requires of us.

For the believer, diligently spending time in the Word is crucial to growing in an intimate relationship with God. If we really want to know the God who we desire to please, it is not enough to listen to the Word being delivered by others; we must have our own intimate time with God daily in His Word.

Also, if we want to give our hearts to the Lord, having knowledge of His Word will build our faith in Him; faith in God comes by hearing and meditating on His Word.

The aim of this book is to point you to the Scriptures by introducing you to God's commands and how you can apply them to your lives, as seen in the lives of His servants.

This book will help to build a desire in you for a deeper relationship with God. It will also help to point you to the Word of God so you can know more about Him. I charge you not to believe the deception that it is satisfactory to just have a shallow and lukewarm relationship with God; you were made for more, so dig deep and seek Him with all your heart. Do not be daunted by your current circumstances; the Holy Spirit will help you to draw closer to Him each day.

Above all, to every believer, please read the Word of God to get to know Him. This is our first point of reference in desiring the truth of God.

Preface

Having accepted Jesus Christ as my Lord and Savior in my late teen years, I thought I had a fairly good idea of what it meant to be a Christian (outwardly). In fact, the very moment I said yes to the Lord, I thought I would have a good feeling, and my broken heart would be fully healed. However, after weeks, months, and then years of feeling this deep void, my spirit was made aware that there is a need to draw closer to God each day.

The Lord then started this great work in my heart by first pointing out to me that I needed to seek Him more. He would give hints, and I can recall Him speaking through my peers at University. He would send persons who helped to sharpen the desire for Him in my heart; they would randomly ask questions about my walk with God and His purpose for my life. At the time I had no idea what was happening in my heart; I was saying in my mind, "What are you talking about?" But it was God beginning His work in my heart.

I began to act on this desire for God by attending campus Bible study and socializing with children of God on campus who were burning for Him. He further joined me to mature believers who were discipling me personally to grow in my relationship with God and to help others to grow as well. After these encounters, I saw God not as someone who was far off but as someone who wants to draw near to us (See Jeremiah 29:13).

God wants to have an intimate relationship with us and to have intimate exchanges with His children. I further saw where being intimate with His Word drew me closer to Him. In **John 1:1** it says the

Word is God, so spending time in the Word gave me the opportunity to see God for Who He is and exposed me to some of His thoughts and expectations for my life. We can never fully comprehend God because His ways and thoughts are higher but spending time in His Word gives us a picture of who He is and His expectations for us.

The Holy Spirit is the one who helps us daily to draw close to God and to feast on His Word.

Have a Relationship with God

Chapter One
First Thing: Seek and Find

"And you will seek Me and find Me,
when you search for Me with all your heart."
(Jeremiah 29:13 – NKJV).

I had this episode in my life where I was so busy and distracted with activities that left me drained. There were many signs in my heart that told me that my life was off balance and I needed to refocus my time. I got this simple alert when I was going through some wallpapers on the internet to add to my phone. I came across one that said, "Return to Me with all your heart." I was immediately shaken into the reality that I had drifted from a consistent focus on God to pursue other things.

God gives us this beautiful promise, if we seek Him with all our hearts, we will find Him. "All" means our everything; all our effort, all our mind, and all our soul, holding nothing back in our pursuit of God. It is like having a goal and setting all plans and resources in place to chase that goal. God deserves to have our whole heart, not a part of it. He should be our number one priority; no one else should hold that place in our lives. There are so many things happening around us, even our own pursuits, that can distract us from pursuing a relationship with God. However, now is the time to make every effort to build a closer walk with the Lord.

> God deserves to have our whole heart, not a part of it

Seek His Kingdom First

Living in this world where our physical needs are highlighted and seem so immediate, it can be daunting to think we have to "put them aside" so we can pursue God's kingdom. However, life is more than just satisfying physical needs.

> *Therefore I say unto you, Take no thought for your life, what ye shall eat, or what ye shall drink; nor yet for your body, what ye shall put on. Is not the life more than meat, and the body than raiment? (For after all these things do the Gentiles seek:) for your heavenly Father knoweth that ye have need of all these things. But seek ye first the kingdom of God, and his righteousness; and all these things shall be added unto you. (Matthew 6:25,32-33 – KJV).*

God does care about our needs; He genuinely cares. Look at the detail in which He describes His ability and willingness to provide for us. Look at how He feeds the birds without much effort on their part; we are much more valuable than the birds. So, do not think we are the only ones who are concerned about our total wellbeing. God knew us first and thought about us long before we knew about ourselves. God is clearly stating that we do not know how to fully provide for ourselves, He does, so we should not allow fears about our future provision to hinder us from seeking God first. There is already enough that we worry about; seek God first and allow Him to take care of what you worry about.

When we seek God, this ensures that we do not miss out on the substance of life, that very purpose that God created us for. There are so many instances where we go before God and do not consult His will or desires for our lives, and then our lives go off the course God intended it to go. Right now, God is encouraging us to get back to the place where we seek

Him first and then allow everything to fall into place. This involves a focused vision of God, His desires, and with a view of eternity. We must remember that these few years we get on earth are just a speck of time compared to eternity; therefore, our decisions now should have an eternal view; knowing that there is always something greater in store with a dedicated focus on our walk with God.

Focus On His Plans For You

Additionally, another way we can get distracted from God is by focusing on what is happening in the lives of others. We should look to God for direction for our lives, not other people. When we look to others, there is a high possibility that we will miss what God tailored for us. There are times when we can seek direction from others, based on the leading of the Holy Spirit, which is beneficial. However, we should not blindly follow in the footsteps of others just because what they are doing looks good. We may end up being totally derailed, especially if that person we are emulating is not walking in God's purpose for his/her life.

See "My Desire" (A Poem by Debra-Kay Williams) in the Appendix.

Chapter Two
To Pray Or Not To Pray

What Is Prayer?

This definition of prayer is a favorite and taken from the book *"Arise, Intercessors Arise!"*: "Prayer is a friend spending time talking with another friend, and that is God" (Rev Dr. Maria L. Harbajan, 2015). This definition gives us a primary reason to pray, that is, to spend time talking to God. It sounds simple, but that is the main reason we should pray. God desires to hear our own voice, talking to Him, not necessarily to ask for anything for our personal gain but just spending time with Him, getting to know Him. Have you ever noticed that some persons only talk to some people when they want them to give them something, but they completely ignore them other times? We should treat God better than that; He wants to engage us on a level deeper than just us asking Him for things.

Why Is It So Hard To Pray?

And he went a little farther, and fell on his face, and prayed, saying, O my Father, if it be possible, let this cup pass from me: nevertheless not as I will, but as thou wilt. And he cometh unto the disciples, and findeth them asleep, and saith unto Peter, What, could ye not watch with me one hour? Watch and pray, that ye enter not into temptation: the spirit indeed is willing, but the flesh is weak. (Matthew 26:39-41 - KJV).

So, we have established that it is important for us to pray, but we agree that it is sometimes challenging to do so. It takes a special grace from the Holy Spirit to commit to a personal time of prayer. The truth is, we must contend with the weaknesses of the flesh to have a consistent prayer life. Such weaknesses include sleep, busyness, personal desire for pleasure and just not being able to find the inspiration to pray. God is very aware of all these weaknesses of the flesh as mentioned by Jesus Christ; this is where the Holy Spirit comes in; He will propel us to seek the Lord in prayer. In **Galatians 5**, we learn that there is a constant war between the flesh and the Spirit; when we lose this war to the flesh, we are kept from doing God's will.

In this age of social media and trying to keep up with the latest trends, there is a long list of other things we could identify that draws our attention away from seeking the Lord through prayer. These are some of the things that have caused us to fall asleep and become very nonchalant in our approach to prayer.

Some of us have given up completely on praying for ourselves and have handed over that responsibility to others, always asking others to pray for us. While it is good to pray for others in love, it is important that each person practice praying because it is an avenue through which we will learn the voice of the Lord.

We must move from seeing prayer as just a thing we do when we feel like or when we want something. We should see prayer more as something that God instituted so we can have open communication with Him through Jesus Christ. This is so amazing: the God of the entire universe made a way where we can talk to Him. He specifically set aside an open line of communication to Himself. That is the faithful God whose ears are open to our prayers. We may not be able to reach the most dedicated family member or friend at every moment when we need them, but we can reach the Lord at any time and on any day of the week. He does not go on vacation from His people; what a faithful God!

How Should We Pray?

Before praying and having an encounter with God, our hearts must be in the right place. He sets out the conditions under which we meet with Him. So, a searching must take place in our hearts, allowing the Holy Spirit to highlight anything in us that displeases Him, and we should then allow Him to remove everything that He does not want to see in us. A major hindrance to us going to God in prayer is unforgiveness in our own hearts; we must overcome this before we enter sweet communion with God.

> *And when ye stand praying, forgive, if ye have ought against any: that your Father also which is in heaven may forgive you your trespasses. But if ye do not forgive, neither will your Father which is in heaven forgive your trespasses. (Mark 11:25-26 - KJV).*

Types Of Prayers

Praise

Psalm 89:8 says: "O LORD God of hosts, who is mighty like You, O LORD? Your faithfulness also surrounds You." (NKJV).

This prayer involves acknowledging God for who He is (as described by Him in the scriptures) and exalting Him in that identity. We can practice this type of prayer by reflecting on His nature and verbalizing our adoration to Him.

Waiting

Isaiah 40:31 says: "But those who wait on the Lord shall renew their strength; They shall mount up with wings like eagles, they shall run and not be weary, they shall walk and not faint." (NKJV).

This is quieting our hearts before God and resting in Him. This discipline is very necessary so that our spirits can be renewed in Him.

Praying The Scripture

James 4:3 says: "You ask and do not receive, because you ask amiss, that you may spend it on your pleasures." (NKJV).

The scriptures are God's promises, and He is bound by His faithfulness to perform His Word. Praying according to scripture (God's will) is key to ensuring that our desires are in alignment with what God wants to perform.

Intercession

This type of prayer involves standing in the gap for someone or speaking up (praying for) someone who needs support or intervention on their part. We should practice this out of love for others with a genuine desire to see the person being helped. This type of prayer reveals those who genuinely love their neighbors, because it gives us the opportunity to stand up for the weak.

Sometimes the Lord gives us a burden to pray for nations and the unsaved; we should be obedient to Him and allow the Holy Spirit to teach us how to pray.

Example: Abraham praying for Sodom and Gomorrah (Nation)

In **Genesis 18**, Abraham goes to God on behalf of the nation of Sodom, pleading with Him to withhold His hand of judgment from them. God made Abraham aware of His impending judgment on Sodom, and even though Abraham may have seen all that Sodom did to warrant God's judgment against them, that did not prevent him from persistently seeking God for some mercy on that nation. God revealed His intention to Abraham regarding Sodom; essentially, God had no obligation to inform Abraham of His plans, and he did not just take this as mere information. Abraham used it as an opportunity to intercede on behalf of the nation. Similarly, God can reveal to us His intention to bring judgment on a nation; our role should be to seek God for His mercy on that nation and allow Him to make the final decision.

And the Lord said, Because the cry of Sodom and Gomorrah is great, and because their sin is very grievous; I will go down now, and see whether they have done altogether according to the cry of it, which is come unto me; and if not, I will know. And the men turned their faces from thence, and went toward Sodom: but Abraham stood yet before the Lord. And Abraham drew near, and said, Wilt thou also destroy the righteous with the wicked? Peradventure there be fifty righteous within the city: wilt thou also destroy and not spare the place for the fifty righteous that are therein? That be far from thee to do after this manner, to slay the righteous with the wicked: and that the righteous should be as the wicked, that be far from thee: Shall not the Judge of all the earth do right? (Genesis 18:20-25 - KJV).

Jesus Interceding For His Disciples (Friends)

In **John 17**, Jesus Christ makes a passionate intercession for His disciples. Jesus brought the deep concerns of His heart to the Father to intervene in the life of His disciples. From this time of intercession, we see the unbreakable connection between the Father and Son, and we also see the love that Jesus Christ has for His disciples. We should also pattern this form of love and deep concern for our loved ones when we intercede for them. It is key for us to intercede on behalf of others facing challenges or those who have a challenge in praying for themselves. This type of prayer helps to build the body of Christ and may also help the believer who is struggling in their relationship with God.

Sanctify them through thy truth: thy word is truth. As thou hast sent me into the world, even so have I also sent them into the world. And for their sakes I sanctify myself, that they also might be sanctified through the truth. Neither pray I for these alone, but for them also which shall believe on me through their word; That they all may be one; as thou, Father, art in me, and I in thee, that they also may be one in us: that the world may believe that thou hast sent me. (John 17:17-2 - KJV).

<u>Singing</u>

This can be prayer that is spontaneous and inspired by our recognition of who God is and what He has done for us. This can also involve us singing the scriptures to God in our prayer time.

There is an example of a prayer sung to God in **Judges 5**. Here the Judge, Deborah, was singing a song of victory, honoring and exalting God for His mighty hand that defeated Israel's enemy, Canaan. This song expresses God's attributes of being the omnipotent

One who defended His people. This song also acknowledges the Lord God as the Author of creation, whose very presence commands the attention of nature. A song of praise is something that we should practice each day. This is also a good way to incorporate scripture in our lives daily. This type of prayer also helps to keep us awake and focused in our times of reflection.

Moses And Aaron

This too is an example of singing prayers of praise unto God:

> *Then sang Moses and the children of Israel this song unto the Lord, and spake, saying, I will sing unto the Lord, for he hath triumphed gloriously: the horse and his rider hath he thrown into the sea. The Lord is my strength and song, and he is become my salvation: he is my God, and I will prepare him an habitation; my father's God, and I will exalt him.*

The Lord is a man of war: the Lord is his name. (Exodus 15:1-3 - KJV).

Listening

Yes, this is a type of prayer and should be practiced more frequently. This happens when we quiet our hearts before God and listen for His personal word for us or for His instruction.

Petition

Philippians 4:6 says: "Be anxious for nothing, but in everything by prayer and supplication, with thanksgiving, let your requests be made known to God." (NKJV).

This is making our requests for physical provision and otherwise known to God with the expectancy that He will provide.

Prayer Is Where Battles Are Won

It is important for the communication between God and man to be kept open so He can establish His will here on earth.

Prayer is not just a thing people do; prayer is agreeing with God to ask for His intervention regarding the concerns He has placed on our hearts.

In Jeremiah 33:3, God instructs us to pray. He said, "Call to Me, and I will answer you, and show you great and mighty things, which you do not know." (NKJV).

This is an assurance that God will act on our sincere requests to Him. He is the God Who can do the impossible, and we are encouraged in scripture to make requests of Him to provide an answer to our most difficult problems. God is promising us that when we pray, He will answer and show us things that we have never seen happen. He will perform the work that exceeds our expectations. This scripture shows us that God has the power to accomplish things that are impossible for us do, and we invite God's hand in the situation when we call on Him (pray).

We can look at the example of Elijah's victory on Mount Carmel. There was a dilemma: the people of Israel turned away from God and were following an idol. Elijah had to step in to prove to the people that there is only one God, and the only way that this could be done was if God Himself showed up. Elijah called out to the Lord to reveal Himself as the true God by sending fire from heaven to consume the sacrifice that was laid for Him. This was to show all the people and the false prophets that there is only one God and that is Jehovah.

> *And it came to pass at the time of the offering of the evening sacrifice, that Elijah the prophet came near, and said, Lord God of Abraham, Isaac, and of Israel, let it be known this day that thou art God in Israel, and that I am thy servant, and that I have done all these things at thy word. Hear me, O Lord, hear me, that this people may know that thou art the Lord God, and*

that thou hast turned their heart back again. Then the fire of the Lord fell, and consumed the burnt sacrifice, and the wood, and the stones, and the dust, and licked up the water that was in the trench. (1 Kings 18:36-38 - KJV).

This is a reminder to us that when we allow God to work and fight our battles through prayer, He will step in and do what we cannot do. Furthermore, our battles are not fought physically, but spiritually and that is why we need to be in prayer so the weapons of the enemy can be destroyed before they are manifested physically. So, the next time we encounter a problem that seems insurmountable, we should call on the Lord who will hear and deliver us.

Chapter Three
Obedience, God's Love Language

Being in a loving relationship with God requires our obedience; keeping God's commandments shows Him that we love Him. We see this in **John 14:15**, which says, "If you love Me, keep My commandments." (NKJV). This shows that God is looking for authentic love that honors His Word. When He looks on our actions, He must interpret them as loving towards Him. Being obedient is essential to the believer's life. It is not only rule-following or strictly following laws, but it is an acknowledgment in one's heart of God's sovereignty, goodness, and love for us. It takes a humble and loving heart towards God to be obedient to Him.

Shema

A further look at obedience to God, based on the command given to the children of Israel, brings us to the Shema. The **Shema** is a daily prayer commanded to be recited by the children of Israel in the Torah (the first five books of the Bible). This prayer is a reminder to the Jews that they should love the Lord with their complete being and reminds them of all the blessings of God that will follow because of their obedience. The Hebrew word "Shema" can be translated to mean "hearing and obeying." This is seen further in **Deuteronomy 6:4-6**: "Hear, O Israel: The Lord our God, the Lord is one! You shall love the Lord your God with all your heart, with all your soul, and with all your strength. And these words which I command you today shall be in your heart." (NKJV).

We see that obedience is not just following rules but a response in love towards who God is and what He requires. He expects a complete response in our hearts to Him, a total surrendering of our will to His. God still expects this form of uncommon obedience today. Obedience, therefore, should not be a shackle but our bond or promise of love to the King.

Partial Obedience Is Not Sufficient

Another aspect of obedience is for us to fully obey instructions given. Since obedience involves fully surrendering ourselves, it follows that we must surrender our own wisdom and what we think is right to fully trust what God says and act on His desires. It is saying yes to God, not considering the consequences or being afraid of attempting what He has asked us to do. We must ensure that we carry out the instructions when He asks us to do it. If we follow His specific instructions, we will surely please Him and benefit from the blessings He has for us.

There is the case of a man called Saul who was a king in his time, who God gave some specific instructions to totally destroy the enemies of Israel, the Amalekites. However, Saul refused to obey the voice of God and instead was moved by what the crowd wanted and spared some of Israel's enemies.

We Fail

We can admit that sometimes we fail God by not obeying Him fully and putting our own desires before His. A lot of us have this struggle if we are being honest, and we also struggle to let go fully and allow the Lord to lead our lives. Note that disobedience is not just breaking one of the ten commandments as we know, but disobedience is any rebellion to God's will, all His commands: spoken and written.

Disobedience hurts: it hurts God, and it also hurts us. God, in His intent, desires for man to dwell with Him and have unending fellowship, like Adam and Eve before the fall. However, we saw where that fellowship was broken because of disobedience and sin. Similarly, when we sin against God, it creates a wall in our relationship with Him, which leaves us feeling empty and sad.

Consequences Of Disobedience

One of the main consequences we face because of disobedience is not being able to dwell in God's presence. Seeing that the human soul cannot find rest outside of God, we see where this can be very painful for us. Therefore, when we are straying from God, we have this void in our hearts and feel empty and lost. Adam and Eve had a firsthand experience of this when they were taken out of God's presence because of their disobedience.

Sometimes, this affects us, and we feel far away from God when we have strayed from Him. We must ensure that we seek the Lord and ask for His forgiveness.

When God Hides His Face

> *And the heathen shall know that the house of Israel went into captivity for their iniquity: because they trespassed against me, therefore hid I my face from them, and gave them into the hand of their enemies: so fell they all by the sword. According to their uncleanness and according to their transgressions have I done unto them, and hid my face from them. (Ezekiel 39:23-24 - KJV).*

Our sins can cause God to hide His face from us. We see this example in scripture more than once when His people were separated from Him because of their sins. In this case, the Israelites were unfaithful to God and sinned against Him. As a result of their sins, God hid His face from them, and they were delivered to their enemies. This is something for us as believers to ponder: do we really know what we risk losing when we are disobedient to God? Our disobedience or sin does not benefit anyone; not us and not God. We saw the devastating effect it had on mankind when Adam and Eve sinned against God. He responded then by putting Adam and Eve out from the garden of Eden and His presence; that can still happen today. If we choose to continue sinning without genuine repentance, we may lose the treasure of communing with God. If intimacy with God is a priority for us, then we know that not being able to talk with Him freely is quite a burden to bear.

Chapter Four
True Intimacy

That Deep Longing
(Jeremiah 29:13)

This is one of the greatest promises that God has made to us, that is, if we seek Him diligently with our whole hearts, we will find Him. Having a heart that seeks after God is a treasured thing; a heart that burns for God and is sick when not close to God's presence. God has built this desire in us for Him; this is necessary for us to make that first push to want to be with Him. Have you ever had the urge to eat your favorite dessert but then realize that you had to visit at least ten stores before you could find that yummy treat? Or, even more serious, you are in a situation where you have not had food for days; how much would you search or how far would you go to ensure that your body gets the desired food it needs to survive? This is the type of desperation we should seek God with because He is more able to sustain and satisfy us than the food our body needs. Jesus Christ is everything we will ever need to fill us up.

We should be like a deer; they open their mouth wide in rapid pants gasping for air when they long to find a source of water. That is how we should gasp in deep breaths with the aim in mind of His presence. The deer seeks to find what it really wants and does not stop until it finds water. We should never stop pursuing God and seeking His face for who He is. It should be our constant push to run after God and have our desires fulfilled in Him.

> *As the deer pants for the water brooks, so pants my soul for You, O God. My soul thirsts for God, for the living God. When shall I come and appear before God? (Psalm 42:1-2 NKJV).*

Did Someone Say Marriage?

It appears that there is an ever-growing desire for marriage by most young women in the church. Many persons have various reasons why they want to get married. For some, it is tradition, security, companionship, a feeling of completeness, and for others, it is a desire for intimacy. It is true, men and women were not meant to be alone. God said it is not good.

> *"And the LORD God said, "It is not good that man should be alone; I will make him a helper comparable to him." (Genesis 2:18 - NKJV).*

God created us to be in relationships, whether it is in a family, with friends, church fellowship, or work associates; at all stages in our lives, we are in some form of relationship. So, it is natural for us to want to spend the rest of our days here on earth with someone who is exclusively committed to us.

"Therefore a man shall leave his father and mother and be joined to his wife, and they shall become one flesh." (Genesis 2:24 –NJKV).

Before we gaze off into deep fantasy about being married, we should be mindful that no matter how much we like to be social and be around people, we want to be alone sometimes. We all need our personal time of reflection and quietness. These times are priceless and precious, especially when spent with God. We should note that no matter how close a person is to us, they will never be able to satisfy us like Jesus Christ can. He can reach and fully satisfy our hearts; He can touch the hidden places in our hearts. The relationship with God will also outlast our earthly marriage; it will be for eternity. This helps to fix our heart's posture on developing a relationship with God because that is the only relationship that will last forever.

Jesus Christ made a commitment to His children that He will never leave or forsake us.

The vow that is traditionally made between a man and a woman on their wedding day: "until death do us part," does not apply to our relationship with God. Death cannot separate born-again believers in Jesus Christ from God; He still remembers us even in death and will faithfully raise us up, as He promised, to spend eternity with Him.

> *"For I am persuaded, that neither death, nor life, nor angels, nor principalities, nor powers, nor things present, nor things to come, nor height, nor depth, nor any other creature, shall be able to separate us from the love of God, which is in Christ Jesus our Lord." (Romans 8:38-39 – NKJV).*

Get In His Presence

What does it take to get into the presence of God? Do we have to lose things sometimes to get close to Him? Sometimes God invites us into His presence, but when He does, it is based on His terms. Let us look at the example of Moses in **Exodus 3**. Moses was invited to Mount Horeb to meet with God. However, before Moses could get close to God, He gave him an instruction to remove his sandals as he was entering holy ground. That holy ground is where God is. He has requirements for us before we can get close to Him. Moses had on different pieces of clothing, but He told Moses what he needed to take off. Similarly, God will instruct us on what we need to let go of to get close to Him. We also see where Moses eagerly complied because He wanted to get close to God.

So, God's invitation must be matched by our obedience and our willingness to let go of some things. Moses did not hesitate; he did not ask why; he just complied, and God invited him to speak with Him from a close place. If you want to move from the outskirts or move from speaking to God from afar, we must comply and accept His invitation to come to Him because He has to draw us to Himself. We must fulfill all the conditions He requires to get close to Him. If someone invites us to be guests in their home, they have conditions, and we must comply with the conditions for the communication to be unhindered and be comfortable in someone's personal space. What is God asking us to let go of so we can get close to Him? Is it something that we are doing that is not pleasing to Him, or could it be that our associations do not facilitate the freedom for us to go deeper in God? We need to assess our lives and hearts to see if there is anything in us that would hinder our level of intimacy with God.

The Holy Spirit will help to detect anything that hinders us from being in a relationship with God. He wants us to come close to Him because He wants to commune with us as His child. So, let us not be afraid to let go of things to gain the prize of intimacy with God. It means we must assess everything we deem as valuable. Is it worth it: letting go of an earthly treasure to get close to God? Look at Moses; he was in the company of many other Israelites, aiming to go to the same place. However, God pulled Moses aside for a purpose. He pulled him away from the crowd and drew him to Himself. God will pull us away from things that are distracting, so our attention can be placed on Him.

Face To Face

Intimacy with God is like a friend talking to a friend (See **Exodus 33:11**). This was the experience Moses had when he spoke to God in the tabernacle.

This is the relationship God wants to have with us today. He desires to speak to the man or woman He created in His image; He wants to be close to us. Therefore, He sent His Son to reconnect us to Him by shedding His blood after our sin separated us from the Father. He also sent His Holy Spirit to prompt us to seek His face.

There is just something about two close friends who are in a deep, meaningful relationship, where there is no hindrance to their communication, and they enjoy each other's company.

How close can we be to God? How close do we want to be? This is a question we should all ask ourselves. Is it okay to be labeled as a Christian or a churchgoer who does all the right things? Or is there something more than just living a good life externally for others to see?

God has called us to more than a surface relationship. He has called us to draw close to Him, to be completely consumed in our hearts by His presence, by Himself. There is so much more to be had from a relationship with God. He is so vast, so we will never be able to fully consume all He has to offer. At every stage in our lives, our focus should be fixed on seeking Him, which is an infinite pursuit of God. God wants our attention; that is why He placed this insatiable hunger inside us for more of Him. Some of us mistake that hunger for something else and end up seeking after empty fillers that leave us more lost and confused. Why should we settle for less when God

> God has called us to more than a surface relationship. He has called us to draw close to Him, to be completely consumed in our hearts by His presence, by Himself.

has so much more for us? We sometimes notice after persons have accomplished great achievements, they feel empty soon after. This happens because these achievements cannot fill the deep void in our hearts. It takes something more than degrees, accolades, and being popular to fill our hearts.

God wants to give us the greatest treasure we could ever have: Himself. We can mirror our desperation for something more by looking at the case of the woman at the well and her encounter with Jesus Christ. She was desperate for something more, and in her conversation, Jesus Christ saw what she needed and promised to give her living water that would continually spring up in her into eternal life.

> *"But whoever drinks of the water that I shall give him will never thirst. But the water that I shall give him will become in him a fountain of water*

springing up into everlasting life." The woman said to Him, "Sir, give me this water, that I may not thirst, nor come here to draw." (John 4:14-15 – NKJV).

This shows us that God's presence, poured out in us, is the only thing that can continuously fill us.

What If You Do Not Fit In?

So, you are this hip, cute girl who has many friends and does not want to feel too weird by talking about God all the time, but "You are a chosen generation, a royal priesthood." 1 Peter 2:9 NKJV). God called you for much more than you see around you; that is why you feel so uncomfortable with mediocre living and surface conversations regarding your faith. This can be an indication that God is calling you out into the deep to pursue Him more and truly spend your life seeking His face. This could mean that you must change your circle; you must spend your time with others who have an active burning desire for a deep relationship with Jesus Christ. There is a high possibility that if you continue to turn off that desire to fit in, then your flame will soon go out, or your flame will gradually die out because of a lack of fuel, especially when there is no one around you to motivate you to draw near to God.

Peter, James, And John

Maybe it is time to assess those people who are closest to you. Do they have that burning desire for God? Are they propelling you into that deep walk and fellowship with God? It is good to get into the company of others who have the same desire as you toward God; they will be great motivators to you. These are the people who you can call in your times of deep searching and seeking the Lord's face. You will need these persons who are grounded in faith and who will not hinder or delay your progressive pursuit of God. We see this awesome example with Christ, who knew the people He could call on for support in His times of seeking His Father. This incident is captured in Matthew 26:36-38: *"Then Jesus came with them to a place called Gethsemane, and said to the disciples, "Sit here while I go and pray over there." And He took with Him Peter and the two sons of Zebedee, and He began to be sorrowful and deeply distressed. Then He said to them, "My soul is exceedingly sorrowful, even to death. Stay here and watch with Me." (NKJV).* This is evidence that we need a core group of persons around us who facilitate the seeking.

Knowing God's Heart

Being in the presence of the Lord and drawing close to Him will result in Him revealing Himself to you. Investing your time in His presence will result in Him opening Himself to you by His Spirit, so you can have the great privilege of knowing God deeper. Some may not see this as important and just settle for a life of just knowing about God and not actually knowing Him deeply in their heart. The Lord seeks such to seek Him, to worship Him in Spirit and truth.

> Some may not see this as important and just settle for a life of just knowing about God and not actually knowing Him deeply in their heart.

"But the hour is coming, and now is, when the true worshipers will worship the Father in spirit and truth; for the Father is seeking such to worship Him." (John 4:23 – NKJV).

He wants to be close to His people, and He wants you to know Him.

Revelation

God will visit you and give revelations of Himself; these revelations flow from intimacy with Him. Once we open our hearts to receive God and to know Him, He responds by revealing His mysteries to us. Revelation of God is important if we want to respond to Him correctly and if we desire to truly worship Him for Who He is. Since God's ways are higher than ours, we have to open our hearts to receive what He wants to show us. If we look at John's encounter with the revelation of Jesus Christ (See Revelation 1:9-11), he was in a place to receive revelation from Jesus Christ because his spirit was ready and open to receive from God. If we want a revelation from God, we must be in a place ready to receive Him. That means we should be expectant and constantly maintain that level of intimacy with Jesus Christ to hear from Him.

Prayer

Lord, I seek You above all others, above everything and everyone; You are my heart's desire. Satisfy my soul with Yourself. I seek You above all. In Jesus' name. Amen.

Going Deeper

Chapter Five
How Much Do You Know The Word?

> "It is written, 'Man shall not live by bread alone, but by every word that proceeds from the mouth of God."
> (Matthew 4:4 – NKJV).

This is not just a saying; these words were expressed by God because He knows that people cannot survive merely on physical food. Humans are spiritual beings; therefore, we need spiritual food to survive. Just as our bodies remind us of our need for physical food, the Holy Spirit reminds us of our need to fill our spirits. It is a challenge sometimes for most persons, young and old, to develop a healthy Bible reading lifestyle. In conducting a simple survey of Christians ranging from ages 18-32 years, it was found that 64% of them did not read their Bible every day.

It is true that we struggle to read the Word sometimes, but reading the Word is key to knowing who Jesus Christ is. The Word of God is not like any other writings or just mere words on pages. The Scriptures are divinely inspired by God; "All scripture is God breathed..." (See 2 Timothy 3:16-17).

The Word of God is also beautiful because the Word is God.

> *"In the beginning was the Word, and the Word was with God, and the Word was God. And the Word was made flesh, and dwelt among us, (and we beheld his glory, the glory as of the only begotten of the Father,) full of grace and truth." (John 1:1,14 – KJV).*

Every moment we spend in God's Word, we are getting to know more about this God we serve. This revelation of Him through His Word can only be led by the Holy Spirit. The Holy Spirit will lead us into the truth of who God is in His written Word. If we truly want to know God, we must spend time in the Word. God is not defined by persons' opinions or what persons say about Him; He is defined by what He says about Himself in His Word. It is important for us to spend time in His Word so our own minds and hearts can be filled with the truth of who God is; we sometimes get deceived by persons who have destructive intentions to sway people away from God and draw them to themselves.

Read To Know Him

If a relationship with Jesus Christ is important, our spending time in the Word should not only be for head knowledge but also to get heart knowledge of Him. This means that our pursuit of God should not be an intellectual one to be well versed in His Word, but our pursuit of Him should be fueled by the Holy Spirit who is able to lead us into knowing God's heart. The next time we take up the scriptures, it will be like having a rare opportunity to have access to the heart of God.

> If a relationship with Jesus Christ is important, our spending time in the Word should not only be for head knowledge but also to get heart knowledge of Him.

Hidden Treasure

"Your word I have hidden in my heart, that I might not sin against You." (Psalm 119:11 – NKJV).

There is another key to being in a relationship with God, that is, to have His Word in our hearts. The issues of life flow from our hearts, so if we want to reflect God's character, then our hearts must be changed by His Word, and that work takes consistency in knowing and meditating on His Word. Knowing God's Word is a step in keeping His commandments. The writer of this text realized that he had to be diligent to seek the Lord to keep His commandments. This is crucial for us too, so we are not led away by the various views and opinions that others would have about truth and morality. This is key for all of us who must grapple with the many teachings and ideologies that are bombarding us in the world today. We must ensure that our foundation of faith is not built on the opinions or doctrines of men or the most popular preacher but on the written unchangeable Word of God.

Study To Show Yourself Approved

If we want to be excellent at something, or if we want to know the Word so we can know God, we must invest the time to learn from Him. This is where we spend our time diligently going through the scriptures with the help of the Holy Spirit. We should not do this to receive a badge of honor or to gain respect from men as someone who knows a lot of scripture. However, we should do it as an act of intimate pursuit of the knowledge of God. As it says in **2 Timothy 2:15:** *"Study to shew thyself approved unto God, a workman that needeth not to be ashamed, rightly dividing the word of truth." (KJV).* We are studying to show ourselves approved unto God, who is looking for a sincere diligence in us who seek after Him through His Word.

The Prosperous Way

In a very compelling charge to His servant, Joshua, the Lord made it clear to him that he should obey the law given to him through Moses. God was teaching Joshua about His Word, particularly how to honor His Word and make meditating on it a priority in His life. This is a primary example to us that God takes His Word seriously and does not forget His law. It is interesting that even while the living God of Abraham, Jacob, and Isaac was literally having a verbal conversation with Joshua, He was still reminding him about His written Word. This is amazing! From that time, God has been personally teaching His Word, and we see where Jesus Christ, when He came, taught the Word, and now we see where the Holy Spirit is teaching the Word. So, for all ages, God has been teaching and is still teaching His Word.

"Only be strong and very courageous, that you may observe to do according to all the law which Moses My servant commanded you; do not turn from it to the right hand or to the left, that you may prosper wherever you go. This Book of the Law shall not depart from your mouth, but you shall meditate in it day and night, that you may observe to do according to all that is written in it. For then you will make your way prosperous, and then you will have good success." (Joshua 1:7-8 – NKJV).

Like Joshua, we are reminded to keep the Word of the Lord at the forefront of our minds and meditate on it day and night so we can have true prosperity and success.

Chapter Six
Fasting, Is This Necessary?

Fasting is sometimes a struggle for some and, depending on the type of fast, the level of challenge differs. Fasting is essential to living a life led by the Spirit and helps us to war against the desires of the flesh.

Traditionally, fasting was seen as a thing we should do to get something from God, but can we see fasting as a means by which God can get more of us. Fasting is an avenue through which we can develop intimacy with God. When we fast, we hear less of our carnal thoughts, and our ears become more in tune with the Holy Spirit, so we begin to hear God more clearly.

Fasting is a challenging subject for some, not because persons do not want to fast, but because we see fasting as extremely hard and, for some, impossible.

Fasting is hard; it weakens our flesh, but it is also beautiful because it allows us to depend not on our own strength but on the strength of the Holy Spirit. When we realize our own weaknesses, we are awakened to the strength of the Holy Spirit. We also receive a fresh refill from the Holy Spirit as He comes and communes with us in our time of physical weakness.

Examples In Scripture

So, he was there with the LORD forty days and forty nights; he neither ate bread nor drank water. And He wrote on the tablets the words of the covenant, the Ten Commandments. Now it was so, when Moses came down from Mount Sinai (and the two tablets of the Testimony were in his hand when he came down from the mountain), that Moses did not know that the skin of his face shone while he talked with Him. (Exodus 34:28-29 – NKJV).

In Exodus 24, there is this beautiful exchange that took place between the Lord and Moses.

The Lord invited Moses on top of Mount Sinai to speak with Him and give Moses the law. The Lord appeared to Moses as He promised and revealed Himself to him. This revelation brought Moses to a place of adoration and worship of the Lord.

So, we see that being in the presence of God is like being in paradise. Moses had the experience of his very appearance changing because he spent time with God. When we enter God's presence, we are changed. He changes us with His presence and the beauty of His glory. There is just something glorious about being in God's presence where time just stops. When we fast, we lose all energy from our flesh and must rely on the Holy Spirit for strength.

There are various fasts that we can partake in to get closer to God and draw away from everything else. If you are a beginner, it is important to start fasting gradually and then allow your discipline to develop. For example, you can partake in half day fasts and use that time deliberately to spend in the Word and with God in prayer. Another type of fast we can do is sleep fast, where we forgo a night of sleep or some hours of sleep to spend time in the Word, worship, and in the presence of God. Since God never slumbers or sleep, He deserves the twenty-four hours we have in the day. However, due to the weakness in the flesh on this side of eternity, we should use our waking moments or sacrifice some of our sleep to spend in worship, knowing that we are joining with the angels who never sleep but are around the throne of God singing praises to Him.

Another tool to use to ensure that our time of fasting is effective is a schedule. So, for each hour of fasting, we can write the scriptures that we will focus on or write the specific question we are seeking God for or the specific attribute of God we are focusing on at that time. This is to ensure that each hour of fasting is accounted for and that no time is wasted. Fasting is not effective unless we use the time to spend with God. Otherwise, we will just be starving ourselves from food and wasting time. Fasting should be filled with the Word of God, prayer to God, and worship to God that will invite the presence of God.

There are great rewards to fasting; the main benefit is that our relationship with God is strengthened. So, we should make that sacrifice, invest our time and shift our outlook from spending time with God to get things, to spending time with God to know more about Him, immersing ourselves in Him. Fasting may seem hard, and it is hard to make that sacrifice, but it will be worth it; just push through to the end. Look at how Jesus Christ spent the forty days and nights in the wilderness and endured; then the angels came and ministered to Him. Similarly, when we take the time to weaken our flesh, the Lord will send His Holy Spirit to come and strengthen us.

Fasting Makes Prayer More Focused

Another good thing about fasting is that it makes our prayers more focused. Since fasting is a kind of pulling away from the strength of the flesh and a reliance on the strength of the Holy Spirit, the fervency that we put in our prayers tend to be greater when we fast. In a time of fasting, we are more cognizant of the Spirit's power, and we tend to rely more on Him to help us pray, rather than relying on our own strength.

Fasting Produces Fruitful Results— "Some Do Not Go Out"

There are some strongholds for which we cannot receive breakthrough unless we earnestly seek the Lord through prayer and fasting. So many times, we struggle with prolonged demonic attacks and devices against our lives because we do not spend the time in God's presence to allow Him to adequately prepare us, by the Holy Spirit, to rebuke these attacks.

Lord, have mercy on my son: for he is lunatick, and sore vexed: for ofttimes he falleth into the fire, and oft into the water. And I brought him to thy disciples, and they could not cure him. Then Jesus answered and said, O faithless and perverse generation, how long shall I be with you? how long shall I suffer you? bring him hither to me. And Jesus rebuked the devil; and he departed out of him: and the child was cured from that very hour. Then came the disciples to Jesus apart, and said, Why could not we cast him out? And Jesus said unto them, Because of your unbelief: for verily I say unto you, If ye have faith as a grain of mustard seed, ye shall say unto this mountain, Remove hence to yonder place; and it shall remove; and nothing shall be impossible unto you. Howbeit this kind goeth not out but by prayer and fasting. (Matthew 17:15-21 - KJV).

The time Jesus Christ spent with His Father resulted in His empowerment by the Holy Spirit to do works that were to come. If some go not out except through prayer and fasting, we should practice this lifestyle as children of God, so we are equipped with the Holy Spirit to do the works ordained by God. This also means that we should not despise the time we spend in fasting even when it seems insignificant; we are to diligently seek the face of the Lord because we do not know what we will face ahead.

Chapter Seven
Loving God

God deserves our true love and nothing less. He does not treat us with partial love; He gives all. The type of love He requires is that which truly comes from our hearts to warm His heart. It is not enough to just confess our love for God; we must show Him our affection.

> *Then Mary took a pound of very costly oil of spikenard, anointed the feet of Jesus, and wiped His feet with her hair. And the house was filled with the fragrance of the oil. (John 12:3 –NJKV).*

Mary of Bethany poured out her expensive perfume on the feet of Jesus Christ. She saw this as an expression of her love lavishly poured out on Jesus. How much do we pour out our love for

Him? If we look at this example, in the actual sense, Mary used a large sum of money that was worth one year's wages to purchase the ointment. Think about using the equivalent of that now to purchase perfume; some people and even ourselves may consider it a waste when we could have used that money to purchase some asset or save it to finance our education. We can consider that amount of money as time; can we pour out or give a meaningful amount of time or hours out of our day to God? Time is a type of investment that does not happen by chance, but a decision made to spend time with Him or to spend time in His house serving Him. This expression of love to God shows that He is worthy of our time: a valuable resource that cannot be regained. Some may look on and say that you are too young to be spending your time seeking after God; some would say you should spend your time chasing after dreams or pursuing relationships. However, just as we give time and attention to the things and persons that are seen, we should give that time to God. Let us not consider pouring out our lives and time before God as a waste. If we lay down our lives for God, it does not go unnoticed by Him.

If we consider the use of Mary's hair to wipe the feet of Jesus, we can see that as an act of great humility. A woman's hair is her glory and crown (See 1 Corinthians 11:15). So, symbolically, Mary was laying her crown at the feet of the Son of God, saying that He is worthy of her crown and worship. This is similar to worship that takes place around the throne of God, where the twenty four elders fall before the eternal God and cast their crowns before Him.

"The twenty-four elders fall down before Him who sits on the throne and worship Him who lives forever and ever, and cast their crowns before the throne, saying:

"You are worthy, O Lord,

To receive glory and honor and power;

For You created all things,

And by Your will they exist and were created." (Revelation 4:10-11 – NKJV).

Just imagine kings, governors, prime ministers, and presidents disregarding their posts to worship at the feet of the Lamb. This is the type of selfless love that we are to give to God; a love that is unreserved, that comes from a heart that recognizes who God is and causes the person to burst out with loving actions towards God. How many of us can say that we can do what Mary did? What crowns do we possess today that we can lay at the feet of Jesus? We can also look at Jesus' response to Mary. He was quite receptive to this genuine love that Mary poured out to Him. For when others criticized Mary, Jesus commended her for her act of love towards Him.

But Jesus said, "Let her alone; she has kept this for the day of My burial. For the poor you have with you always, but Me you do not have always." (John 12:7-8 – NKJV).

Chapter Eight
Do You Fear God?

A key part of the journey in a relationship with God is to know who He is. Surely, He has described Himself in His Word, and those are the descriptors that should form our perception of Him. We know that God is truly loving and kind and has the best interest at heart for mankind. That alone could be an aspect of Him that would command our reverence for Him, knowing that He has the power to totally cast us off because of the wickedness of mankind, but He still chooses to extend mercy to us. Also, we know that the Lord God is a consuming fire who has all power to destroy His opposers. This means that there should be reverential fear of God and a loving fear that leads to our total obedience to Him.

Abraham displayed that loving fear of God when God told him to sacrifice his only son Isaac. This was extremely hard for Abraham to do because he waited so long for that promised child, and he loved him so dearly. Abraham was caught in a tough place: he loved God and wanted to be obedient to Him, but he also loved the son God gave to Him. We see the challenge that may have arisen in Abraham's heart in this situation; however, he proceeded to obey the Lord, not knowing the full extent of what God wanted to do. Abraham trusted God in this difficult moment; he trusted the heart of God enough to know that once He gave him a command, he should obey.

Now it came to pass after these things that God tested Abraham, and said to him, "Abraham!" And he said, "Here I am." Then He said, "Take now your son, your only son Isaac, whom you love, and go to the land of Moriah, and offer him there as a burnt offering on one of the mountains of which I shall tell you." (Genesis 22:1-2 – NKJV).

Some of us may be able to relate to this incident: God asking us to do something, and we deem it difficult. We may delay and ask God to give us a hint or to show us what is coming ahead with His instruction. However, we can learn from Abraham's encounter with God; we do not have to get any explanation from God about what He wants to accomplish with any instruction He gives us. It is expected of us, who are in a loving and close relationship with God, to trust His counsel, knowing that anything He asks us to do is not arbitrarily done but something that He would have thought through. There are so many times that we disobey God out of the fear of the unknown, but we should obey God out of fear and love for Him, for who He is and what He wants to accomplish.

Then they came to the place of which God had told him. And Abraham built an altar there and placed the wood in order; and he bound Isaac his son and laid him on the altar, upon the wood. And Abraham stretched out his hand and took the knife to slay his son. (Genesis 22:9-10 – NKJV).

Despite how Abraham may have felt, he did not consider his feelings above obeying God. He saw it more important to hear and obey God's instructions rather than succumbing to his fleeting feelings. This is the type of submission we should give to God: a form of submission that says "yes" to Him, even though we do not know what is coming on the other end of His instruction. This may not be so easy to do, but the grace of God is enough to help us to act out our love for Him. Abraham would have seen the value of obeying God and would have proceeded despite his feelings. We can be left with two important lessons from this encounter: the fear of God happens when we take His Word for what it is, and the fear of God is where wisdom begins.

Daily Steps

Chapter Nine
Make Time To Meet With God

As children of God, we have a longing to be alone with God and have desires that only He alone can fill. If we do not spend time alone with Him, we can feel lonely and empty. God has placed this void in our hearts, and the only way that void can be filled is if we make time to be with God. When we make time to do other things that are deemed important, such as, studying, spending time with friends, and scrolling through social media, these activities only drain us and leave us empty. We must make the same commitment to God; He is our Father, and He is a real person who desires our attention.

When we spend alone time with God, we are refueled, we are refilled, and our hearts are mended into wholeness, allowing us to look more like Him each day. If we examine our natural relations, like dating, we realize that both parties must spend time with each other so they can get to understand each other. As more time is spent together, they will understand the values and expectations of each other. Similarly, when we spend time with God, we get to understand what He likes or does not like. The Word of God contains His thoughts, and we can get to know His thoughts by making time to read the Word.

One way to make the time to meet with God is to develop a schedule; it is more likely for us to commit to a time when we make a schedule. This is similar to schedules we make for class, interviews, and travel. This means we must be consistent to benefit from the time we dedicate to be alone with God. It involves setting an actual appointment and sticking to it. The moment we do this, we realize how God honors appointments set with Him because He will come and commune with us.

What should we do when we spend time with God? The first thing to do is to talk to Him through prayer. Prayer is talking to God. God is our Father, and He wants to hear from us; He is interested in everything we have on our minds. God is omniscient, but He likes us to speak to Him, like a child talking to a loving father. He invites us in **Jeremiah 33:3** to call to Him, and He will answer us and show us great and mighty things which we do not know.

The second thing we should do is to spend time reading the Word. The Word of God is His thoughts expressed in written form, as He expressed Himself in the person of Jesus Christ, who is also the living Word. We must meditate on scripture and allow the Holy Spirit to speak to our hearts. When we do so, we will be surprised how much He reveals to us in our quiet time. This will not happen by chance; we must commit the time to hear from Him. We make an appointment to visit the hairdresser and have to go and spend time in the salon chair to get our hair done. If we want a deeper relationship with God, we must stick to our commitment to spend time with Him.

Another thing we can do in our intimate time with God is to worship Him. Worship is our response to God's glory, beauty, and majesty. It is difficult for a person to be in the presence of God and not worship; we can journal our thoughts towards Him, write poetry and sing songs in our heart that come from His revelation of Himself to us.

We have an example of a person who pulled away to be with the Father; this person is Jesus Christ. There are many occasions noted in the gospels where Jesus pulled away to be with His Father. There seems to be something that Jesus saw when He spent time with His Father, and there was something that constantly pulled Him away to be with God. A key example is recorded in Matthew Chapter 4 where Jesus Christ spent forty days and nights in the wilderness.

"Then Jesus was led up by the Spirit into the wilderness to be tempted by the devil. And when He had fasted forty days and forty nights, afterward He was hungry." (Matthew 4:1-2 – NKJV).

It was a challenging time for Jesus, but when Jesus came out of that time spent with the Father and using the Word, He was strengthened to overcome the attacks of the enemy. After that period of pulling away, Jesus Christ was strengthened to walk in His ministry here on earth.

God recognizes our smallest efforts to spend time with Him. Even though we think we have many things to do, it is still worth much to spend time with God despite the other things vying for our attention. There can be times where we must hide or forgo some activities or invitations just to be alone with Him. The Holy Spirit draws us to Him because God has a purpose for pulling us away, and there is a work in our hearts He wants to perform. Sometimes this can only be done effectively when we spend time alone with Him.

Another lesson from the wilderness experience is that Jesus did not break the time allotted to spend time with God. We must not break the time we commit to spending with Him, even though "life" is happening. Even in Jesus' case, there may have been persons who needed ministry, and persons would have wanted to speak with Him, even His friends. However, He did what the Holy

Spirit instructed Him to do. There may be times when God is asking us to spend one day, three days, twenty-one days, or however long alone with Him, and we may feel like we cannot do it because there are so many persons who want our attention and there are so many persons we want to talk to. However, just be obedient and spend the time God wants you to spend alone with Him. God will be pleased when we obey His commands. If we do not spend the allotted time in His presence, the work that He wants us to do will be delayed. Additionally, the assignments He has for us for a particular season will be delayed too. Do not be concerned about what others may think; just be concerned about what God wants you to do. If He wants you to set aside a particular time, just do so.

"Now after six days Jesus took Peter, James, and John his brother, led them up on a high mountain by themselves;

and He was transfigured before them. His face shone like the sun, and His clothes became as white as the light." (Matthew 17:1-2 – NKJV).

There are other times that Jesus spent alone with the Father, and He manifested Himself to His Son. Sometimes God wants to reveal parts of Himself to us and will only do so in times when we are alone, just like Moses was alone seeking the Lord, and God passed by Him in the cleft of the rock and showed Moses His back. When the Lord wants to give revelation, He sets the conditions under which He reveals Himself to us. Sometimes that condition is that we make the time to be alone with Him. I have often spent time examining the relationship between fathers and daughters. Based on my observation, the daughters who spend time with their fathers and have conversations with them are closer to their fathers.

Even with other relationships, we can see where parties involved must spend time with each other to get to know each other and trust each other with their hearts and secrets. For the relationship to grow, those parties must become unguarded around each other. The way we get unguarded is to spend more time with that individual and be more comfortable with them. The more time we spend with them, the more we can test their commitment to us and the relationship. The more comfortable you become, the more you will begin to share more of yourself with that person, sharing areas that are not shared with others. If we desire intimacy with God, we cannot just pass by Him, but we must dwell in His presence daily.

A great benefit of spending time with the Lord is that we hear Him more clearly. For us to develop the focus on God's voice, it involves tuning out all distractions, including the destructive thoughts we have in our own minds. In spending time with Him, we are able to discern His voice and learn what He speaks. It is important for us to learn the voice of God so we can walk in the direction and path He has for our lives. As He says: "My sheep hear My voice, and I know them, and they follow Me." (John 10:27 – KJV). Hearing His voice does not only have to do with seeking direction for our lives, but it is important in order for us to commune with God daily. When Christ was on earth, He dwelt in God's presence. He never only sought God when He had a particular assignment or had something to do; He sought God as a habit. We need to be in God's presence to survive. Imagine how hard it would be for us as believers to live, if we are not hearing God's voice, and imagine how difficult it would be for Christ to be sent here on earth and not commune with God daily. If we commune with Him daily, we will be able to hear His voice.

Chapter Ten
Give Yourself To Him

Is there anything in your life that God has asked you to surrender to Him, and you think it too hard to give up? God is asking for more than a profession of Him; He wants more commitment from you; He wants you. We should not have God as a side option or as someone we run to for things or temporary comfort. There are some gifts that God has given us that He is requiring for Himself to be used for His glory and for His kingdom. Further, there are

> God is asking for more than a profession of Him; He wants more commitment from you; He wants you.

some possessions that God has given us that He now requires for His use. He also wants to use some positions He has given us to occupy so His Name can be exalted. Are we willing to give up the things and titles that we value so much so God can have His way in our lives?

Additionally, God gave those good gifts, and they are not above Himself, His desires, and His will for us. Even a Queen gave up her position to honor God and His Word in her life. That is, Queen Hadassah (Esther). She was formally an orphan who was raised by her cousin, Mordecai, in Shushan. She was later promoted to queen in place of Vashti, who was removed from her role as queen when she refused to go to her husband, King Ahasuerus, when he called her.

> *"On the seventh day, when the heart of the king was merry with wine, he commanded Mehuman, Biztha, Harbona, Bigtha, Abagtha, Zethar, and Carcas, seven eunuchs who served in the presence of King Ahasuerus, to*

bring Queen Vashti before the king, wearing her royal crown, in order to show her beauty to the people and the officials, for she was beautiful to behold. But Queen Vashti refused to come at the king's command brought by his eunuchs; therefore, the king was furious, and his anger burned within him." (Esther 1:10-12 – NJKV).

There was a royal decree made in the kingdom for young virgins to be brought to the palace for the king to choose a queen.

"Then the king's servants who attended him said: "Let beautiful young virgins be sought for the king; and let the king appoint officers in all the provinces of his kingdom, that they may gather all the beautiful young virgins to Shushan the citadel, into the women's quarters, under the custody of Hegai the king's eunuch, custodian of the women. And let beauty preparations be given them." (Esther 2:2-3 – NKJV).

Esther, who was favored by God, was chosen as queen. She was put in this position by God, but God had a plan. Esther may have just seen the part of the story where she was a chosen queen, and then that would just be it. Then came a conflict, where Haman, one of the king's princes and enemy of the Jews, instigated a decree to destroy Esther's people.

> *"Then Haman said to King Ahasuerus, "There is a certain people scattered and dispersed among the people in all the provinces of your kingdom; their laws are different from all other people's, and they do not keep the king's laws. Therefore it is not fitting for the king to let them remain. If it pleases the king, let a decree be written that they be destroyed, and I will pay ten thousand talents of silver into the hands of those who do the work, to bring it into the king's treasuries." (Esther 3:8-9 – NKJV).*

Somehow, Esther was in the perfect position of influence to intervene to save her people. Possibly, Esther never saw this coming, but God had this in mind from the beginning. God raised her up as a queen for such a time, to stand up for her people, to save their lives. Esther had a huge obstacle to cross; attempting to go before the king to stop the destruction of her people could have cost her life.

> *"All the king's servants and the people of the king's provinces know that any man or woman who goes into the inner court to the king, who has not been called, he has but one law: put all to death, except the one to whom the king holds out the golden scepter, that he may live. Yet I myself have not been called to go into the king these thirty days." (Esther 4:11 – NKJV).*

Similarly, God may be asking us to do something that seems impossible, that may cost us our positions and even our lives. When we see obstacles, we tend to come up with reasons why we cannot act on God's instruction. Our lack of willingness may be a fear of letting go of what we have, yet we should recognize that the God in our lives is far bigger than anything He has given us. Pleasing God is worth much more than holding on to what we treasure here on earth.

There are times when giving ourselves to God seems so hard, but it is important that we seek God's counsel whenever we feel like it is too hard to do something that He has called us to do. If we withdraw and ponder the matter to ourselves, then we may delay obeying God's command. Also, if we consult others who are not led by God, we may end up doing the opposite of what God requires. The key is to always keep communicating with

God regarding any matter concerning our lives. He has the master plan for us, and He will give directions on how we, in partnership with Him, can execute those plans in our lives.

Full Surrender

Even though it was challenging for Esther to risk her life to go before the king, she did it anyway. She may have had a battle with God internally, considering the risk that she was about to take. Nevertheless, she pushed forward with faith in God for His hand in the deliverance of His people. Esther made a bold move in calling a three-day fast to seek God's intervention on the matter.

God does not want a part of us but all of us. Sometimes we must turn away from popular opinion and seek God for His direction in our lives. We should not settle to do what seems easy or manageable for the time and neglect to give all that God has called us to surrender to please Him.

Finally, we should give our hearts to the Lord. When He has that, He has our everything. He deserves to have all of us, and it should be our pleasure to surrender ourselves to Him.

Appendix

Poem: "My Desire"

My heart beats for You, my lungs gasps for the breath of Your Spirit, my heart cries, my soul sings, it is You that I want; the only One, the only One who can satisfy me.

I wait in earnest fasting; I am hungry for You, Yahweh. I seek You in prayer. I call to You, I cry to You, only You will satisfy this longing, this searching. So, all my days I will seek You, and in the night watches, I will wait on You.

My heart leaps in the glory of Your presence. This is my desire: to gaze at Your beauty, to give You my daily offering of praise and my gazes in the wonder of Your majesty. Oh, for Your deep touch to reach my soul; for You to revive me with just a drop of Living Water.

Then my soul will rejoice with new melodies, and my voice will explode with new songs, with high praises unto Yahweh, Who satisfies me.

Forevermore this will be my anthem: that my soul needs You. I will not rest, but I will run after You all my days, and my banner will be "Yahweh, You are welcomed here." My soul will find her rest in You.

References

- **Chapter 2** Types of Prayer: International School of Ministry-Workbook 2

- **Chapter 3** Shema definition:
https://www.myjewishlearning.com/article/the-shema/

- **Chapter 4** True Intimacy:
https://petalsbloom.com/why-jesus-is-better-than-a-husband/

  Definition for Prayer: Harbajan, M. L. (2015) Arise… Intercessors Arise!: A Manual For the Birthing, Calling, Training and Restoration of Prayer Warriors. Outskirts Press, Inc.

About the Author

Debra-Kay Williams is a daughter of God who has a heart for missions. She also has a deep desire to know God, which is expressed in her keen interest in studying the Word. She is currently pursuing a Diploma in Ministry with the International School of Ministry, and she loves the idea of small group Bible study. She holds a Bachelor's Degree in Business Administration and is active in student ministry. She has the vision of seeing young people desiring God deeply while on campus and in life generally. She has a passion for writing. She often journals, writes poetry and blogs.

www.ingramcontent.com/pod-product-compliance
Lightning Source LLC
Chambersburg PA
CBHW071138090426
42736CB00012B/2151